The Ways of the Winds

Contents

What to Do

<u>YOU MIGHT NEED:</u>
- a dictionary
- a thesaurus
- an atlas

<u>NOW:</u>
- choose a face
- when you see your face, you are the leader
- when you are the leader, follow these steps:

1. Predict

Say to your group:
"I think this page is going to be about..."

You can use these things to help you predict:
- photographs
- captions
- headings
- what you already know

Tell your group to read the page silently.

2. Clarify

When your group has finished reading, ask them if there is anything they don't understand.
Say: *"Is there anything anyone doesn't understand?"*

It could be:
- a word
- something someone has read

3. Ask Questions

Ask your group if anyone would like to ask a question about what they have read.
Say: *"Does anyone have a question they would like to ask?"*

4. Summarize

Now... you can tell your group what the main ideas are on this page.
Say: *"I think this page has been about..."*

What Is Wind?

I predict this is going to be about…

Wind can cause problems…

The wind is like the Earth's breath. We can't see it or hold it, but we can see and feel its effects. It can be an incredible force, a wonder of nature that can shape our lives in many ways.

Sometimes the wind can be light and gentle, like a summer breeze. This is the wind that can fan us and keep us cool on hot days.

Sometimes it is roaring and swirling, moving at a devastating speed. This is the wind that can tear down buildings and rip up trees, leaving a path of destruction.

Wind is simply part of life on Earth – sometimes as friend and sometimes as foe.

Does anyone need to have anything clarified?

... but it can also be useful.

Does anyone have a question to ask?

My summary of what we have read is...

Learning About the Wind

Ancient People

I predict this is going to be about...

Ancient people could see that there was a great force in the movement of wind. Although they had no real understanding of it, they realized they could use this force. More than 5,000 years ago, the ancient Egyptians learned to use the force of the wind to sail on the Nile River. It is thought that the ancient Persians built the first windmill more than 2,000 years ago.

Roman farmers used the wind to help them separate the part of the wheat they couldn't eat – the chaff – from the part they could.

They spread the wheat on a floor, and on a windy day, tossed it in the air with pitchforks. Because the chaff was lighter, the wind would blow it away. The edible part of the wheat would fall to the floor.

Does anyone need to have anything clarified?

The Nile River, Egypt

Today, wind is not needed for harvesting wheat.

Ancient Greeks

I predict this is going to be about...

The ancient Greeks were mostly farmers and sailors, so the wind played a big role in their lives.

The ancient Greeks thought the wind came from a cave or from the four corners of the Earth. They believed the wind had special power, and that it was made up of eight gods. There was a god for each direction the wind blew from, and each one had a name and a face.

The north wind was like an old man with shaggy hair and a beard. He was harsh, and he brought winter. The south wind brought the hot winds and storms of late summer, and he was feared as a destroyer of crops. The east wind was thought to be unlucky, even though he brought warmth and rain. The west wind was the gentlest of winds. The other gods represented winds from the northeast, southeast, northwest, and southwest.

STOP

When you read, "the south wind...was feared as a destroyer of crops," what picture do you get in your head?

Does anyone need to have anything clarified?

The First Weather Vane

I predict this is going to be about…

Boreas – the north wind

The Greeks realized they could study the wind's directions to learn about weather patterns. They built a marble tower with a weather vane on top to measure wind direction.

The tower was shaped like an octagon and was called the Tower of the Winds. Each face had a carving of one of the eight wind gods. The weather vane on top was a Greek god named Triton, who had the head and body of a man and the tail of a fish. As the wind turned this huge vane, the finger would point in the direction from which the wind was blowing. This was probably the first weather vane, and the tower still stands today.

Does anyone need to have anything clarified?

The Tower of the Winds – the weather vane is gone, but the tower still stands.

Early Explorers

I predict this is going to be about…

More than 1,000 years ago, Vikings were the first explorers to sail far out of sight of land. To cross the open ocean, they had to learn new ways to navigate, including using the ocean's wind systems, which blow in huge "wind circles."

In later years, Portuguese explorers learned how to avoid sailing into the doldrums – the place where the winds are calm. If their ships sailed there, they could get stuck, and the crew might die from lack of food and water. Sometimes when the gale winds blew ships off course, explorers discovered new lands.

After a while, sailors discovered the trade winds. These winds helped open a pathway over the ocean. Ships followed this pathway to explore the world for trade and to find new lands to live in.

STOP
What connections can you make with learning something new?

Does anyone need to have anything clarified?

A Viking longship

A 17th century map, showing the direction of the winds

AB ÆQVINOCTIALI LINEA, AD CIRCVLV POLI A̅
TARCTICI.

Does anyone have a
question to ask?

My summary of what
we have read is...

What We Know Now

I predict this is going to be about...

We have learned a lot about wind since those early days. We know now that wind is air that moves.

The sun heats the Earth's surface unevenly, and some areas are warmer than others. When air gets warm, it rises, and cooler air then moves in to take its place. This moving air is wind. Different seasons bring different winds, winds blow at different speeds, and all winds blow in circles.

There are the major winds, easterly and westerly, that blow around the Earth, carrying the weather patterns. Other winds blow only in one small place. The shape of the land can change the wind's speed. Mountain passes and ocean coastlines can be windier environments.

Does anyone need to have anything clarified?

High-level winds

Low-level winds

A Great Wind

I predict this is going to be about...

Hurricanes are the strongest of the windy storms. These are some of the most frightening, destructive storms on Earth. They form over warm ocean waters. Just like smoke is sucked up a chimney, hurricanes draw warm, moist air off the sea and start spinning around a calm center called an eye. The more air they suck up, the faster they spin and the more furious they become. While the eye of the hurricane can be calm and clear, the eye wall around it is the most violent part.

When hurricanes hit land, they are at their most dangerous. Their massive energy can destroy houses and buildings, uproot trees, and make debris fly like uncontrolled missiles. The wind energy from one hurricane equals half of the electrical energy the entire world can produce!

STOP

When you read, "fly like uncontrolled missiles," what picture do you get in your head?

Does anyone need to have anything clarified?

A huge hurricane moves toward land.

A Small Wind

I predict this is going to be about...

While hurricanes are known for their fast, powerful winds, windstorms called tornadoes can blow twice that fast.

A dust devil is a tiny tornado that sucks up dust, sand, or soil. Dust devils blow in only one small place, and even though they are not seen as very dangerous, they can be a serious hazard for planes. They form mostly on hot, dry afternoons. The ground heats up during the day and warms the air just above the surface. The air begins to swirl around and around, faster and faster, like a spinning top. Almost as soon as it has begun, however, it is over.

Dust devils are common in dry and desert landscapes on Earth – and even on Mars.

STOP

When you read, "like a spinning top," what picture do you get in your head?

18

Does anyone need to have anything clarified?

Dust devils can cause plane crashes.

Dust devils are small winds, but they can be deadly.

Does anyone have a question to ask?

My summary of what we have read is...

Measuring Wind

I predict this is going to be about...

The weather vane idea that ancient Greeks first used is still used today to show the wind's direction. Today, however, a weather vane is usually a simple arrow. The arrow can be connected to a weather station to give the exact direction of the wind. The weather vane must be high above the ground and away from objects, such as buildings and trees, that could affect the wind direction.

A windsock also shows what direction the wind is coming from, as well as how strong it is blowing. A windsock fills with air and points in the direction the wind is going. When there is a strong wind, the sock points out straight, but when the wind is light, it hangs loose.

Windsocks are important tools at airports, because they help show pilots which way and how strong the wind is blowing. This helps them with takeoffs and landings.

Does anyone need to have anything clarified?

A windsock

A weather vane shows us where the wind is blowing from.

Does anyone have a question to ask?

My summary of what we have read is...

I predict this is going to be about...

A weather balloon carries instruments high above the Earth. These instruments then gather information about the weather. As scientists track how and where the balloon travels, they get information about the wind. The balloon uses special radios to communicate with a computer on Earth. Special weather balloons are sent up when there is a hurricane. They send back important information that can let weather forecasters predict what the hurricane might do.

An anemometer is an instrument that measures the speed or the strength of wind. It is important to know how fast wind is blowing before its power can be used. People can use the energy in moving wind to generate electricity, but they must first know the wind's speed.

Does anyone need to have anything clarified?

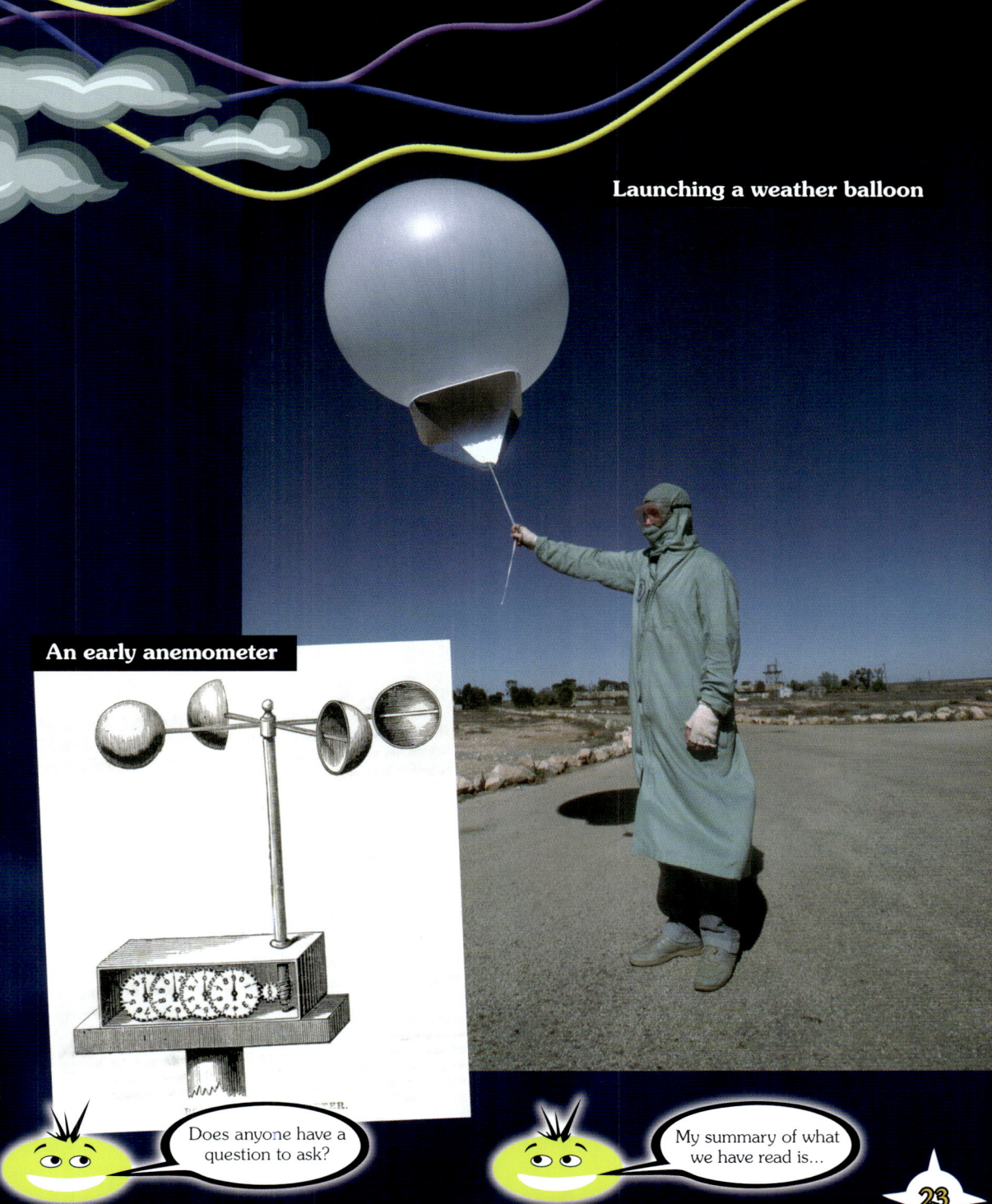

Launching a weather balloon

An early anemometer

Does anyone have a question to ask?

My summary of what we have read is...

Using the Wind

I predict this is going to be about...

While people have used the wind as a power source for a long time, today one of the most important ways to use wind is to make electricity.

A wind turbine is a machine that makes electricity by capturing the force of the wind. It has blades and a shaft. As the wind blows, it turns the blades and the shaft spins. The shaft is connected to a generator that makes electricity. One small wind turbine can make enough power for a home or a school.

However, a lot more electricity can be made when many turbines are grouped together. A collection of turbines in the same place is called a wind farm. Wind farms work best in places where the wind is strong and steady.

STOP

OPINION

More use should be made of the wind. Why? Why not?

Does anyone need to have anything clarified?

One type of wind turbine

A wind farm

25

Wind in Space

I predict this is going to be about...

Wind doesn't just blow on Earth – it blows in space as well. Wind in space is called solar wind, and every planet in our solar system is exposed to it. Solar wind is wind coming off the sun. The solar wind is extremely fast, moving at more than 3 million miles per hour. It can affect spacecraft routes, and even change the direction of comet tails!

As on Earth, there is also wind created by the sun's heat on other planets. The wind on Mars is mostly calm, but sometimes there are dust storms where the wind can gust up to 90 miles an hour. However, because the air around Mars is so thin, even a fast wind doesn't feel as strong as it would on Earth.

Wind is called renewable energy because it will continue to be produced as long as the sun shines. By studying this remarkable wonder, scientists can learn more about our world.

Does anyone need to have anything clarified?

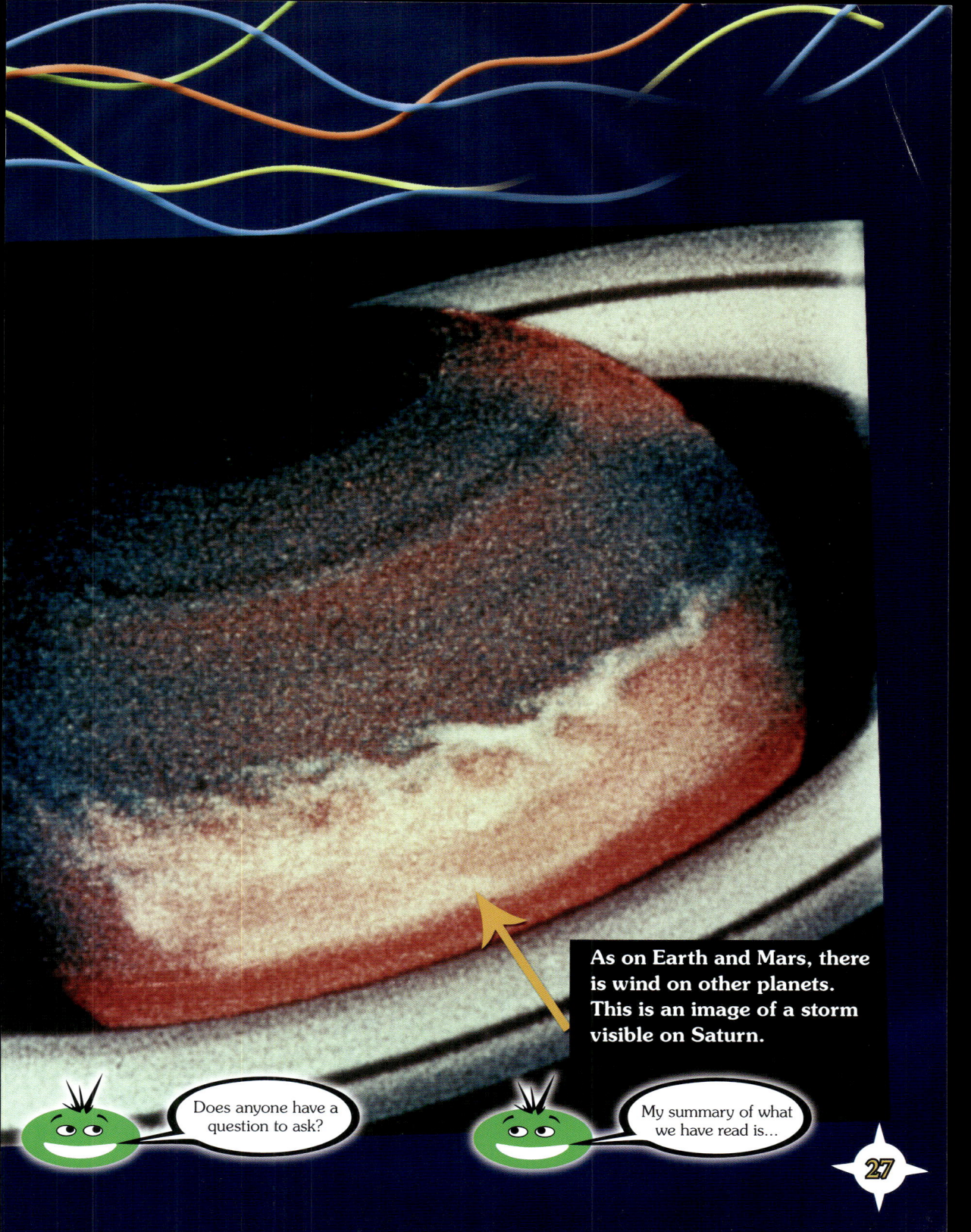

As on Earth and Mars, there is wind on other planets. This is an image of a storm visible on Saturn.

Does anyone have a question to ask?

My summary of what we have read is...

Something to Think About

K

What I KNEW
– before reading
the book

?

L

What I have
LEARNED
– from reading
the book

?

W

What I WOULD
LIKE to learn
– after reading
the book

Ancient
People

The Wonder
of the Winds

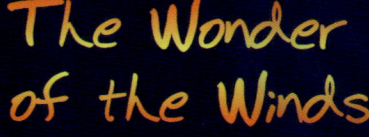

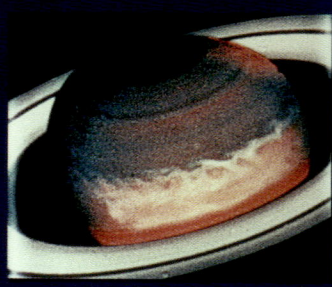

Want to Find Out More?

Try searching in books and on the Internet using these key words to help you:

dust devil
gods of the winds
hurricanes
trade winds
weather balloon
weather patterns
wind farm
windmills
windsock
wind turbine

Index